My Day in the
CITY

Jory Randall

PowerKiDS press.

New York

Published in 2010 by The Rosen Publishing Group, Inc.
29 East 21st Street, New York, NY 10010

First Edition

Editor: Joanne Randolph
Book Design: Julio Gil
Photo Researcher: Jessica Gerweck

Photo Credits: Cover Hola Images/Getty Images; p. 5 © Anna Peisl/zefa/Corbis; p. 7 ©Steve Prezant/ Corbis; p. 9 Douglas Todd/Getty Images; p. 11 Mitchell Funk/Getty Images; p. 13 © Atlantide Phototravel/Corbis; pp. 15, 24 (top left) © Paul Hardy/Corbis; pp. 17, 24 (top right) Shutterstock. com; p. 19 © Tony Arruza/Corbis; p. 21 © Paul Barton/Corbis; p. 23 Ariel Skelly/Getty Images; p. 24 (bottom left) © www.iStockphoto.com/Cheng Chang; p. 24 (bottom right) Bryce Pincham/Getty Images.

Library of Congress Cataloging-in-Publication Data

Randall, Jory.
   My day in the city / Jory Randall. — 1st ed.
      p. cm. — (A kid's life)
   Includes index.
   ISBN 978-1-4042-8075-5 (library binding) — ISBN 978-1-4358-2469-0 (pbk.) —
ISBN 978-1-4358-2470-6 (6-pack)
   1. Cities and towns—Juvenile literature. I. Title.
   HT152.R36 2010
   307.76—dc22
                                    2008051395

Manufactured in the United States of America

Contents

Visiting the city is fun. There is so much to see and do!

I like to climb to the top of a **skyscraper** when I go to the city. Look how far you can see!

Walking down the busy city streets is fun. There are always lots of people, cars, and shops.

I like to ice-skate in the park when I go to the city. Does the city near you have ice-skating?

I like to visit the children's **museum** in the city. There is always something new to learn!

13

The city's natural-history museum is the museum I like best. You can see **dinosaur** bones up close.

On hot days, some city parks have water **fountains**. These are fun places to cool off.

My family and I watch a baseball game in the city. Have you ever been to a baseball game?

The part I like best about a day in the city is lunch! We buy a hot dog from a cart on the sidewalk.

I had a great day in the city.
I hope we come back soon!

Words to Know

dinosaur

fountain

museum

skyscrapers

Index

Web Sites

Due to the changing nature of Internet links, PowerKids Press has developed an online list of Web sites related to the subject of this book. This site is updated regularly. Please use this link to access the list:
www.powerkidslinks.com/kidlife/city/